Youth
Character Building
Toolkit

For organizations, parents, coaches, teachers, administrators

If we want our children to possess the traits of character we most admire, we need to teach them what those traits are and why they deserve both admiration and allegiance. Children must learn to identify the forms and content of those traits.

William J. Bennett, former
U.S. Secretary of Education

Initial research support provided by the United
States Golf Association and Keepers of the
Game

Photos and illustrations courtesy of Pixabay

Published by Denro Classics an imprint of
Collective Wisdom, Inc.
Printed in the United States of America
1700 Mukilteo Speedway, #201 PMB 1084
Mukilteo WA 98275

Library of Congress Control Number:
2018901353

ISBN-13: 978-0-9998667-0-2

Introduction

Welcome to the toolkit that will help you with one of the most important tasks adults can do for the next generation.

Life isn't easy growing up. The average kid can have a tough time of it: being picked on sometimes, is scared, behind at school on occasion, hides a few things from parents, worries about keeping friends and is graded from sunup to sundown.

The average kid also loves telling jokes, dreams about the future, is proud of accomplishments, and is learning new things all the time.

The average kid grows up to be a parent, a clock-puncher, a budget-maker, someone who grocery shops a couple of times a week. The average kid grows up to be an average adult.

Not every American child can earn a Harvard degree and become president. Not every child can become the CEO of an international corporation. That doesn't matter. We don't need everyone to be heroic; we only need each one to contribute to his or her best ability. Every child can become a confident adult, a person who contributes in meaningful ways to the betterment of mankind.

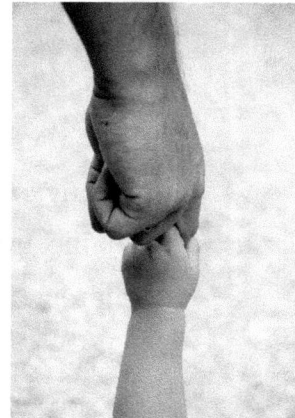

We adults have an important responsibility; to do what we can to help regular kids grow up strong and honorable, and to do this right. Knowing what to do is the first and most important step in achieving this goal.

This toolkit is an introduction to values and character with brief descriptions of how character can develop through any activity and looks at sports and golf as an example of how the elements of an activity can be identified and emphasized. It also includes a list of organizations and books that are good resources for more information.

The toolkit is designed to help you understand the value of systematically evaluating any type of youth program so you can determine if it is doing what is available and possible to enhance the development of character.

Some programs, of course, are not focused much on character development. These programs may be most interested in teaching a skill or participating in an activity, like music or baseball, or simply giving kids something to do while waiting to be picked up by a parent. At the same time, other organizations, such as "Y" programs and The First Tee, emphasize character growth. Our idea is that any program can be designed to positively impact youth character development. All that is necessary is to know what to do and create good ways of doing it.

This toolkit will enable you to understand the character development elements of a program, evaluate how well they are functioning, and guide you to making improvements where you can.

Our philosophy is that youth groups are a fertile arena for significant growth opportunities. Why not take advantage of the best thinking of how to grow our kids in the best way?

Thank you for your efforts and we wish you well.

Contents

Character

We all become something when we grow up: cooks, crooks, golfers, gofers. What we become is greatly determined by our character. How our society functions is determined by our collective character.

To most people, character is "how you act when you think no one is looking." Researchers in the field define it as "acting according to core universal values." Basically, a person of good character has developed a core value system and behaves in a way that reflects that value system. Character is both attitude and behavior.

The group Character Counts! Coalition lists the core values of good character as:

Trustworthiness	Respect
Responsibility	Fairness
Caring	Citizenship

Is character important? Character determined if your physician cheated to pass a few medical school classes. Character determines if someone runs a red light or stops in time. It separates those who you can trust from those you cannot. It emphasizes fairness and caring in a world that is tough, cruel, and uncompromising.

Most, if not all of the core values necessary for good character development are contained in most youth organization's activities from sports to chess to jazz ensembles and include:

Acceptance	Self-reliance
Honor	Concern for others
Responsibility	Integrity
Honesty	Fairness
Respect	Self-control
Excellence	Effort

Like all core values, these do not become part of character by osmosis. Character development is a complicated process for it is not learned all at once nor is it constant in all situations. The concept is that children grow from an external reference of good behavior to an internal one; and that a positive internal reference must be learned.

Youth can easily learn the difference between good and evil. Learning how to be unselfish is much harder. Even more difficult is choosing between two rights; for example protecting a friend in trouble or informing authorities of the friend's behavior.

The right values must become part of the belief system, be used in making decisions and influencing behavior.

There is some uncertainty about when it is best to teach character, but there is no harm in exposing young children to the ideas and considerable benefit helping pre-teens make value decisions. Learning and acting for the greater good is a life-long task.

We in youth programs have the opportunity to enhance how young people grow. We can significantly improve the acquisition of good core values through our programs. However, it is not a simple, nor an easy process.

Activities

Any youth activity has the opportunity to encourage or enrich character development. Kids don't grow character much while watching TV, but by doing things, learning things, being faced with difficult decisions. The more teachers, coaches and leaders can identify and manage these activities, the more likely good character development will result.

Individual activities, like learning to play the cello are wonderful opportunities to help character development. The discipline to practice is a character virtue, as is learning to harmonize with others.

Some activities, such as golf, demand less physical conditioning or absolute athleticism than other sports. Golf still requires all the character elements necessary for success in sports and in the larger world. But it has one element of character building missing almost everywhere else.

The self-policing component of golf adds a critical dimension. It is seemingly archaic that at the professional level golfers are required to be responsible for their own scores. Yet relying on the honesty of the player demonstrates that even at the highest level, only the golfer truly knows how many swings were made during play.

In golf, every element of the game arises from the simple principle that golf is nothing if not a game of honor. Thus, golf, perhaps more than any other sport, can build character. Like other activities, however, neglect of this core element produces a similar sad result: players who value only winning.

Youth golf programs can provide participants with invaluable exposure to the game's core values. These values can be taught, modeled by staff,

experienced during play, reviewed after the game
and even translated into guides for daily living.

Other activities such as model building, music, rock
climbing and even video games may also have
defining characteristics that can be used to display
how important character, recognizing strengths
and weaknesses, and making the right decisions
can be.

Activities that involve teamwork, including working
together on a project provides an environment
filled with opportunities. For example, learning
when to listen and when to speak out is one of the
critical components of being a good citizen. This
can be experienced in any number of ways, from
planning how to play a game, to when to call a rules
infraction to giving feedback to a teammate.

In addition, learning to take direction from others,
responding to authority and fitting into a team can
also be reinforced through many activities.

The key is for leaders to recognize learning
opportunities, discuss and reflect on them, and
help participants understand options and the value
of making good decisions. Sports activities are a
good example of what is possible and can be used
to model what other activities can achieve.

Sports

Much of the character-building elements of sports come from the immediacy of results. Trying hard, overcoming obstacles, teamwork, selflessness, self-reliance and a host of other elements are experienced during play. Scoring or not scoring, winning or losing, season averages and records also can impact character development.

The benefit of sports in building character is that adversity on the playing field is a safe place to learn some of life's harder lessons. Character values can be learned a little at a time and under the supportive guidance of motivating role models. The give and take of teamwork can be fun, instructive, and productive. Coping with disappointment can be put in perspective and the lesson used to do better next time.

However, the demands to win and the complex expectations of organized programs make it difficult for the participant to easily see the benefit of honorable play if doing so lessens the chances of victory. Some research has shown that athletes view playing within the rules to mean doing whatever the officials allow or don't notice. Coaches promote playing hard, dehumanizing opponent to some degree. Sports can build character, but it can also weaken it.

Many of the lessons in sports come from the reaction of adults: leaders, parents, spectators, and coaches. All are involved, knowingly or not, knowledgeable or not. Adults must be very sure of their role, that of an encourager, and not become emotionally involved in the details of play. Coaches coach, parents watch, officials officiate, and kids play.

We can use one sports activity, golf, to clarify how a specific activity can be constructed to promote character development.

In the survey section is a form specific to golf. You may want to create one specific to your program activities.

Teamwork

There is no "I" in team, but there sure is in "win."
What does that mean? It means nothing. Well-meaning, hard-working individuals make up
teams; the best teams are comprised so the total is
greater than the sum of its parts. This does not
mean anyone gives up individuality to be on the
team. What it means is that individuals are
enhanced by the team and the team is enhanced by
the combination of individuals.

*Although the team itself will win and lose, the
experience of being on a team can always be a
positive one for the team member.*

One of the best team-building models is the one
created by Rudy F. Williams, Ph.D., called the
Four-Part Teaming Model.

Part one of the model is a compelling task. This
means that the goal of the team, the vision, the
reason for the team's existence is significantly
important to each team member; important
enough to become a priority. To some, this appears
to be where the team member gives up
individuality for the good of the team. This isn't
what happens. Instead, the team member focuses
on whatever the team needs to succeed. This is
gaining something, team success, rather than

giving up something. Focusing on the team task is an investment, not a sacrifice.

The second part is sense of membership. Each member of the team knows without doubt why he or she is a valued member of the team. And, each member knows without a doubt why each of the other team members is a critical member of the team. Each also knows what he or she is expected to contribute.

The third part is influence on the team. Each member knows how to affect how the team functions, what the rules of interaction are, and what interactive roles each person needs to perform.

Last is personal reward; what is in it for each participant. Often reaching the team's goal is sufficient reward, but others can be important too, such as recognition, learning, awards or payments and prestige.

Team membership can be a significant contributor to character development, especially in the recognition of individual responsibility and accountability toward group success and enduring the public slings and arrows of keeping score.

Building Character through Youth Programs

"Building" character means that we must teach one step at a time over an extended period. We must provide ideas, create learning experiences, and encourage effort. There are ten things we must do if we are going to help young people build character.

1. Have a clear idea (mission) of what we hope to accomplish.
2. Clearly define and explain core values
3. Teach according to the child's developmental level
4. Provide good role models
5. Ensure parental involvement
6. Provide value decision making experiences
7. Measure progress
8. Learn from experience how to improve our efforts
9. Link our efforts with activities outside the organization
10. Make sure leaders are well trained

A parent raising a child may do only three or four of these. A free standing youth program may be able to do them all. Here is more detail on each element.

Mission: The mission is the description of what we want to accomplish. It should be clear and include expected outcomes, roles and responsibilities of all involved, and how everyone will be accountable to meet expectations.

Value messages: The core values are clearly defined and expressed in many ways; through presentations, discussions, modeling, again with clear expectations.

Age appropriate teaching: Program goals, expectations, rewards and consequences are all age appropriate.

Modeling: All adults and older participants are effective role models. Expectations are clear and assessment of effectiveness is made.

Parent/guardian involvement: They are encouraged to be actively involved in planning, running and evaluating the program and expand the value lessons into home life.

Value experiences: Planned and organized experiences expose participants to value decisions. Kids are helped to understand how and why to make good decisions.

Measurement: Participant's growth and the program's effectiveness are both measured.

Improvement: All involved determine how well the program is working and what improvements are needed.

Community links: Program lessons are reinforced and expanded by others, including parents, other youth organizations, and the larger community.

Staff development: Leaders and others constantly seek ways to improve the program and themselves.

Teaching character does not have guaranteed results. The best we can do in increase the probability that our programs help good character develop. The more of these components a program has, the better its chances of instilling the important core values.

Program Assessment

Our effort is to help youth programs assess strengths and weaknesses so all programs have a chance to do their best.

Since measurement of character is difficult, our focus is on the elements of programs, to determine if programs are doing a few or many of the things that are important in character development.

We have taken the ten components of a good program and divided them into specific measurable elements.

Using some or all of the tools, a program can better understand character development within their own organizational structure and make changes that will enable them to better reach their goals.

Our hope is that this assessment method will improve youth programs. Assessment material includes:

- ° Program self-assessment (basic and detailed)
- ° Staff survey   ° Parent survey
- ° Participant survey   ° Community survey
- ° Results sheet   ° Action plan
- ° Comprehensive survey

For new or small programs, the first step would be to review some of the resource material included in this booklet to become more familiar with what others are thinking and doing.

Second, do the self-assessment and staff survey and strengthen any components that can be easily improved. Third, survey parents and participants to identify further improvement opportunities.

For larger or older programs, beginning with the community survey might provide some useful initial insights into how the program is viewed and understood externally. While this is being done, completing the self-assessment and comparing the results to the community survey might also be enlightening.

Then proceed with the other surveys to complete the picture. No matter how you approach evaluating a youth program, make sure it has the necessary basic ingredients. They are:

- Clear value statements
- Value decision making by older youth
- Behavior consequences
- Clear, caring role models

Youth programs should be fun. But unlike informal youth activities, we can provide an enviable foundation in good character values. Enhancing these values while learning and enjoying activities may be the greatest asset for participants.

We must cherish this opportunity and enhance future generations the best way we can.

Books

Beedy, J.P., *Sports PLUS: Positive Learning Using Sports*, New Hampton, NH, Project Adventure, 1997.

Bennett, W.J., (Ed.), *The Book of Virtues for Young People*, Parsippany, NJ, Silver Burdett Press, 1996.

Bredemeier, B and Schields, D., *Character Development and Physical Activity*, Champaign, IL, Human Kinetics Press, 1995.

Brown, Robert, *Personal Wisdom*, Seattle, Denro Classics, 2013.

Gough, R., *Character is Everything: Promoting Ethical Excellence in Sports*, Fort Worth, TX Harcourt Brace, 1997.

Kidder, R., *How Good People Make Tough Choices*, New York, William Morrow, 1995.

Lerner, Richard M. and Benson Peter, *Developmental Assets and Asset-Building Communities*, Springer, 2012.

McNamee, M. and Parry, S., (Eds.), *Ethics and Sport*, New York, Routledge, 1998.

Simon, S., Howe, L. and Kirschenbaum, H., *Values Clarification: a Handbook of Practical Strategies for Teachers and Students,* New York, Hart Publishing Company, 1972.

Thompson, J., *Positive Coaching: Building Character and Self-Esteem Through Sports*, Portola Valley, CA, Warde Publishing Company, 1995.

Yeager, John et al, *Smart Strengths*, New York, Cogent Publishing, 2014.

Books for Parents

Dosick, W., Golden Rules: *The 10 Ethical Values Parents Need to Teach Their Children*, San Francisco, Harper Collins Publishers, 1995.

Eyre, L. and Eyre, R., *Teaching Your Children Values*, New York, Simon & Schuster, 1993.

Lickona, T., *Raising Good Children*, New York, Bantam Books, 1983.

Nicholaus, B. and Lowrie, P., *The Mom and Dad Conversation Piece*, New York, Ballantine Books, 1997.

Unell, B. and Wyckoff, J., *20 Teachable Virtues: Practical Ways to Pass on Lessons of Virtue and Character to Your Children*, New York, Perigee Books, 1995.

Organizations

All About Character, Inc. www.careerstreeterie.org
>P.O. Box 637
>Pleasant Garden, NC 27313
>1-888-BLOCKS-1

Center for the Fourth and Fifth R's www.cortland.edu
>P.O. Box 2000
>SUNY Cortland
>Cortland, NY 13045

Character Education Partnership www.character.org
>1600 K Street NW, Suite 501
>Washington, DC 20006
>800-988-8081

Citizenship Through Sports Alliance
>www.sportsmanship.org

Do Right Foundation www.doright.org
>852 Fiftieth Avenue, Suite 215
>San Diego, CA 92101
>619-235-5634

Ethics Resource Center
>1120 G Street NW
>Washington, DC 20005
>202-737-2258

First Tee   www.thefirsttee.org
>170 Highway A1A North
>Ponte Vedra Beach, FL 32082
>904-940-4300

Giraffe Project   www.giraffe.org
>PO Box 759
>Langley, WA 98260
>360-221-7989

Josephson Institute of Ethics www.josephsoninstitute.org
>4640 Admiralty Way, Suite 1001
>Marina del Ray, CA 90292
>310-306-1868

We worry about what a child will become tomorrow,
yet we forget that he is someone today.

Stacia Tauscher

Licensing Agreement

Purchase of this toolkit provides you and your organization license to use the surveys. This license is limited to one organization within one small geographical area, such as a town, city, or county.

Larger organizations, ones with multiple sites within a state, or national organizations, should use their own judgment as to what is fair and equitable use of the license and buy additional toolkits as appropriate. We suggest purchasing one kit per 50 participants, one kit per physical location, or one kit per major program.

The surveys and worksheets are a good beginning to help you understand how your program is helping kids develop character. Once you have analyzed what is currently working and not working, put together a plan with clear goals, roles and procedures to help you make your program the best it can be.

Simple tools like creating a 3x5 reminder card of role responsibilities for staff can do wonders.

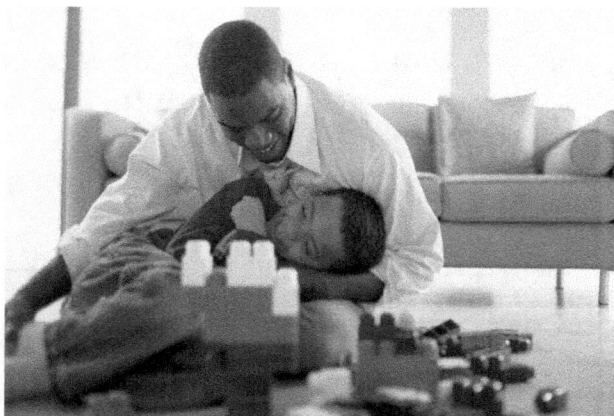

Although analysis and planning can significantly contribute to the impact of any program, ensuring that people who care are the ones interacting with the kids is even more important. Give them the tools and the understanding they need to do the best job.

If you would lift me up you must be on higher ground.

Ralph Waldo Emerson

Using the Surveys

Organizations:

There are three levels: Basic, Detailed, and Comprehensive.

Basic: This level is for small programs with limited staff and resources or for new programs. It is ideal for programs run by 1-5 adults who meet regularly and have clear ideas and agreement on what the program should do and how it should be run. The basic assessment can act as outside eyes to identify and clarify possibilities.

The basic level can also be used to assess individual programs within a larger organization.

Use the basic survey to better understand character building within the program and evaluate what you can do using the Survey Results and Action Plan forms.

Detailed: For most programs, the detailed level should be sufficient to provide a good analysis of current efforts and sufficient information to construct an effective action plan.

Begin with the Detailed Survey form. From those results, an organization can either explore identified weaknesses using some of the questionnaires such as the participant survey, or use all of them for a broader understanding. From this information, the Survey Results and Action Plan forms can be completed, analyzed, and program enhancements initiated.

Comprehensive: For older or highly motivated organizations that are seeking an in-depth analysis. This is the best of outside eyes and critical assessment. It requires an initial self-assessment and a gathering of documents to support that the program is doing what it says it is doing. Then, a person outside the organization who has experience in youth programs uses the survey to guide a review of activities and documents to determine strengths and weaknesses.

The outside expert completes the survey, perhaps also using the other surveys included in the toolkit, fills out the survey summary and comments page, and discusses results with program leadership. At this point an Action Plan can be created.

After this, the detailed survey and the other surveys can be used for continuous evaluations and improvements.

For Parents and Others:

A parent or interested parental representatives can use the detailed survey to interview leaders of an organization to determine how and how well the program supports character development.

The surveys, especially for participants and parents can be used to evaluate those particular elements of a program. Other programs a child may attend can fill out the Outside Organizations survey to determine how well programs are coordinated.

Results should be discussed with others within the program so problems are understood and action plans implemented.

- - - - - - - -

We recommend that you keep hard copies or an electronic file of results so you can have a record and can track your improvements.

Character Building Toolkit

The Kit will help you evaluate how well your program is designed to help participants develop the values that lead to good character development. It also identifies the primary components of an ideal curriculum to help you enhance your program. This kit does not tell you how to run your program, but lists what elements will help participants build good character.

Basic Self-Assessment

Ten item check-list. The program director or others can check "Yes" or "No" on the basic components of a character building program. This should be used by small or new organizations to identify areas that are not part of the program. Those that are not, but of interest, can be further explored using the more detailed surveys or by assessing some of the resources listed earlier in the toolkit.

Detailed Self-Assessment

Each of the basic ten components has been further divided into three elements to give more detail for larger or older programs. These can be used to create policy, define jobs, or to set improvement goals.

Youth Assessment

A questionnaire that can be given to older participants and can be read to or discussed with younger children. This will help staff better understand what messages are being heard by the participants and will help identify the impact of value messages, understanding of learning goals, how well golf values translate to daily living and areas for program improvement.

Staff Assessment

Items designed to have staff identify their understanding of the program and their role in it. Good for all staff, not just those involved in teaching.

Parent Survey

For parents, guardians and others to help determine how much their perspective is part of the program functioning. Will also help determine what their understanding of the program is and how well it is working. Can be used as a discussion tool to help parents understand their role and enable them to contribute to the program in meaningful ways.

Organization Survey

Items to understand how outside organizations picture the golf program. Helpful in understanding image, need for promotion, and possibilities for linkages.

Assessment Summary

A way of organizing survey results so that successful elements are kept in mind, weak areas are identified, priorities are defined, and details from the comments sections of the surveys can be listed. This is the beginning of the improvement process.

Action Plan

One form for each element to be worked on. Follows program management style of identifying issue, defining measurable goal(s), identifying what should be done and also lists necessary resources. The "results" section can become an "issue" for the next improvement effort.

Outside Program Analysis

Detailed program analysis. Should be conducted by trained outside entities. Useful to look at for the amount of component detail and relative weights given for each element. Also a good reminder to have documentation of how the elements are being met, especially so that improvements can be measured.

Youth Program
Basic Self-Assessment

Name of Program _____ Date _____

Your name _____ Position _____

Use this form to identify possible areas of weakness. As you read each item, think about how you know that this exists or happens, and how you measure how well these items are done. Each "yes" answer means that this element exists in the program, can be documented, and those outside the program can easily see how they are done. For any "no's" take a look at some of the resources in the handbook to see if they can help you add the components to your program.

Check right hand columns as appropriate

Component	Yes	No
1. The program has a mission statement that includes helping to develop character values.		
2. Character education is defined as a primary goal of this program.		
3. All participants engage in activities and are disciplined in ways that are age appropriate.		
4. All staff have clearly defined roles and duties that are designed to have impact on participants' acquisition of character values.		
5. Parents and/or guardians are encouraged to participant in different ways.		
6. Learning experiences are clearly defined and reinforced.		
7. There is clearly defined participant accountability.		
8. Efforts are made to improve the program.		
9. The program is linked to other community organizations for the benefit of the participants.		
10. Time and other resources are set aside for staff development.		

Great programs may have only two or three "yes's," but the more your program has, the more likely you are effectively helping your participants to build character.

Youth Program
Detailed Self-Assessment

Name of Program_____ Date _____

Your name_____ Position _____

Component	Element	Yes	No
Mission Statement	1. Published statements define expected behavior of participants.		
	2. Expectations are known and accepted by parents, participants and the community.		
	3. Participants are held accountable to clearly defined values.		
Value Messages	1. Staff exhibit specific behaviors as examples of values.		
	2. All staff activities are defined as value laden.		
	3. There are clearly defined and enforced consequences for inappropriate behavior.		
Teaching	1. Participants are engaged in practicing specific values and values decision-making.		
	2. Targeted results are age appropriate (winning, etiquette, etc.)		
	3. Teaching is individualized according to the needs and developmental stage of each participant.		
Modeling	1. Students perceive the staff as role models.		
	2. All staff have clearly defined roles and duties.		
	3. All staff are evaluated regarding their efforts in providing character developing opportunities.		

Please continue...

Youth Character Development Toolkit

Component	Element	Yes	No
Parent Guardian	1. Parental role is clearly defined.		
	2. Parents receive regular progress reports in various ways.		
	3. Parents can actively participant in aspects of the program.		
Experiences	1. There are clearly defined learning experience and awareness how learning occurred.		
	2. Social rewards are given for expected behavior and discipline is productive rather than demeaning.		
	3. There are frequent discussions and explanations of behavior and consequences.		
Measurement	1. Participants are included in determining targets.		
	2. Baselines are defined and progress measured.		
	3. There is clearly defined staff accountability for outcomes.		
Program Improvement	1. The participants' growth and the program's effectiveness are measured and findings used to improve the program.		
	2. Assessment is focused on progress toward goals and includes input from staff, participants, parents, and the community.		
	3. Measurement includes impact on other life skills.		
Community Links	1. Parents and others are involved in many areas of the program.		
	2. There is regular cooperation between the program and other community resources.		
	3. Lessons from the program are linked to daily living.		
Staff	1. All staff are encouraged to improve skills.		
	2. Warm, supportive relationships are built between participants and staff.		
	3. Praise is the primary motivation tool.		

Youth Golf Program
Participant Survey

Name _____ Age _____

Years playing golf _____ Years in this program _____

1. Circle the four most important things you are supposed to learn in this program.

     Sand shots   The swing   Rules   How to behave

     Etiquette   Putting   Play golf   Driving

2. What is the most fun about this program?

_____

_____

3. Are you learning things that will help you in school or at home?   YES NO DON'T KNOW

4. Are you learning things like playing by the rules,
   honesty, and fairness?   YES NO DON'T KNOW

5. Do the instructors make learning fun?   YES NO DON'T KNOW

6. If you could do this program over again, would you want to? YES NO DON'T KNOW

7. Any suggestions?

_____

_____

_____

_____

_____

_____

Thank you.

Youth Program
Staff Survey

Your name _____Date _____

Your position _____ Years experience in program_____

1. What is your understanding of the youth program's mission?_____

_____

_____

2. What (if any) values does this program teach? How do you know?_____

_____

_____

3. If this program teaches values and helps build character, how does it do that?

_____

_____

_____

4. How is this program's success measured? _____

_____

_____

5. What is your role in teaching values and character development?_____

_____

_____

_____

Please continue...

6. What training or experience have you had in teaching character development?_____

_____

_____

_____

7. What elements of good character do you role model in your job?_____

_____

_____

_____

8. What do you think participants gain most from your efforts? _____

_____

_____

_____

_____

_____

Thank you

Youth Golf Program
Parent/Guardian Survey

Name _____ Date _____

Age of child(ren) in program_____ Do you play golf? YES   NO

1. Circle the four most important things your children learned or will learn in this program.

   Sand shots   The swing   Rules   How to behave

   Etiquette   Putting   Play golf   Driving

5. What is the best feature of this program? _____

   _____

   _____

6. What are some of the rules or expectations of this program? _____

   _____

   _____

Please answer the following on a scale of 5=very much 3= so-so and 1= not at all

7. Is your child learning things that will help in   1   2   3   4   5
   school or at home?

8. Is your child learning things like playing by   1   2   3   4   5
   the rules, honesty, and fairness?

9. How important to you are good character   1   2   3   4   5
   values in sports?

7. Do the instructors seem to care about the   1   2   3   4   5
   students?

Please continue...

8   If you could improve this program, what would you improve?_____

_____

_____

_____

9. Are character values (such as honesty)   YES   NO   DON'T KNOW
    emphasized in this program?

10. Should youth golf programs emphasize   YES   NO   DON'T KNOW
    character values?

11. Do you think that this program will help   YES   NO   DON'T KNOW
    your child develop better life skills?

11. Are you actively involved in running or   YES   NO
    evaluating the program?

12. What values do you think are taught in this program? _____

_____

_____

13. What were the factors that made you choose this program? _____

_____

_____

_____

14. Any suggestions? _____

_____

_____

_____

Thank you.

Youth Program
Other Organizations Survey

Your organization_____ Today's Date _____

Your organization's mission _____

_____

_____

Your name _____

6. What is your understanding of this youth program's mission?_____

_____

_____

7. What, if any, values does the program teach? _____

_____

_____

8. If values are taught, how are they taught? _____

_____

_____

_____

9. How do you measure the youth program's success? _____

_____

_____

10. How is this youth program linked your program? _____

11. How does the youth program work with other community resources?_____

_____

_____

_____

12. How was your organization and others involved in the planning, development and running of the youth program?

_____

_____

_____

_____

_____

13. What do you think participants gain from this youth program?

_____

_____

_____

_____

14.   Any other comments? _____

_____

_____

_____

_____

Thank you

Youth Program
Character Survey Results

Five components /elements ranked highest

1. _____

2. _____

3. _____

4. _____

5. _____

Five Components ranked lowest	Which Survey?	Fix Area ?	What were weaknesses, limitations, etc?
1.			
2.			
3.			
4.			
5.			
Other Findings			
1.			
2.			

Character Survey Results (Example)

Five components /elements ranked highest

1. Published statements defining expected behavior of participants

2. Expectations are known and accepted by parents, participants and the community

3. Parents are involved in may areas of the program

4. Parental roles are clearly defined

5. Parents receive regular progress reports in three ways

Five Components ranked lowest	Which Survey?	Fix Area?	What were weaknesses, limitations, etc?
1. Staff skills improvement	Staff		Part time volunteer staff for only two week period—can encourage, but no time or money to work on this now
2. Baselines are defined and progress measured	Self-assessment	X	Have not taken time to document what kids are like from year to year.
3. Frequent discussions and explanations of behavior and consequences	Self-assessment	X	Half hour period after golf was seen as relaxation time—could have been used for discussion of play.
4. Students perceive staff as role models	Self-assessment	X	Golf pros are great—didn't pay attention to other staff who dress poorly and sometimes yell.
5. All staff activities are defined as value laden	Self-assessment	X	Same as above—did not teach nonprofessional staff that they are part of teaching team.
Other Findings			
1. Logo seems outdated	Community survey	X	Never noticed, got used to it over ten years
2.			

Youth Program
Character Building Action Plan

Issue/Component
/Element
_____
_____
_____

Goal (include
start/finish dates)
_____
_____

Success Measured
By
_____
_____
_____
_____
_____

Actions
_____
_____
_____

Necessary
Resources
_____
_____
_____

Results
_____
_____
_____

Character Building Action Plan (Example)

Issue/Component /Element	Program links to community—only two links in place, few outside golf know of program and efforts to improve character
Goal (include start/finish dates)	Beginning June 1 and with a goal of finishing by September 1, to improve links with other community groups and to improve awareness of the character building aspects of our program within the town and surrounding areas.

Success Measured By	1. Article or articles about the program in the local paper, hopefully with pictures
	
	2. Ten percent increase in informational telephone calls
	
	3. Establish working relationships with:
	   • Boys and Girls Club
	   • Mrs. Jones' Program for Troubled Kids

Actions	Write press releases, call local paper, create flyers Give presentations at local fraternal and social groups and the schools Call local youth organizations, especially B&G club and Mrs. Jones Create new brochure and distribute
Necessary Resources	Someone who can write for flyers, brochures and press releases Funding for materials Set aside time to prepare talks and give them—need examples of program that will engage audience
Results	Four articles in the Bugle two with photos! Twenty-five percent increase in informational phone calls Now actively linked with B&G, Mrs. Jones, the Moose and the Bill Gates Foundation

Youth Program
Comprehensive Program Survey

Program _____

Date _____

Address _____

Surveyor _____ or _____

☐ INTERNAL SURVEY

Organization _____

Telephone _____

Contact person _____

Telephone and e-mail _____

TOTAL POINTS _____   ☐ Met Standard

This survey is to help youth programs assess how well they are providing opportunities for participants to experience and benefit from character building activities. The survey is divided into ten categories, each having separate point totals. Each item in each category is scored at one of four levels with score varying by the importance of the item. It is the program's responsibility to provide documentation for each item scored.

Scoring is as follows: **Does not exist   In development   Exists but unclear   Exists, is clear and effective**

The surveyor will follow the guidelines of documented activities and list how the program meets these guidelines. Activities not listed as guidelines may be documented and scored as appropriate.

Each section has a minimum score for sufficiency in that area.

A score of 100 with all sections meeting the minimum score criteria is necessary to be defined as providing a good program for helping youth develop character. The total number of points possible is 200.

Youth Character Development Toolkit

Mission Statement Documentation / Components	Not Exist	In Dev.	Exists Unclear	Clear Effect.
Published statements define expected behavior of participants			1	2
Mission statement (or character statement) signed by participants and/or parents.		1		2
There is a defined philosophy that guides all aspects of the program			1	2
The discipline code includes character elements.			1	2
Participants are held accountable to defined values.			1	2
Minimum points to pass 5			Pass?	Yes
TOTAL				No
Total possible points 10				
POINTS				

Youth Character Development Toolkit

Clear Value Messages Defining documents	Components	Not Exist	In Dev.	Exists Unclear	Clear Effect.
	Use of examples, historical or local, of character issues.		1	2	3
	Participants encouraged to provide examples of values.		2	3	4
	Staff exhibit specific behaviors as examples of values.		4	6	8
	Character education is defined as a primary value in the educational process.		2	4	5
	There are clearly defined consequences for inappropriate behavior.		1	2	4
	Consequences are enforced for inappropriate behavior.		1	2	4
	Character elements are used as part of the overall definition of "winning."			1	2
	Minimum points to pass 15				
	TOTAL			Pass?	Yes
	Total possible points 30				No
	POINTS				

Youth Character Development Toolkit

Age appropriate teaching Documentation	Components	Not Exist	In Dev.	Exists Unclear	Clear Effect.
	Participants are expected to exhibit specific value behaviors.		1	3	5
	Participants are engaged in practicing specific values and values decision making.		2	5	8
	Participants receive specific values feedback.		1	2	3
	Outcome emphasis is age appropriate (winning, fun, skill development, honor, self-confidence, teamwork, self-reliance, etc.)		1	3	5
	Participants have a feeling of safety and support.		1	2	3
	Teaching is individualized according to the needs and developmental stage of each participant.		1	2	3
	Individual participants have a file or other record that is used to determine needs and document progress.		1	2	3
	Minimum points to pass 14				
	TOTAL			Pass?	Yes
	Total possible points 30				No
	POINTS				

Youth Character Development Toolkit

Modeling Documentation	Components	Not Exist	In Dev.	Exists Unclear	Clear Effect.
	All staff have clearly defined roles and duties.		3	7	10
	Students perceive the staff as role models.		3	7	10
	All staff are evaluated for their efforts in providing character development opportunities.		3	4	5
	External "high profile" models are bought in as examples and to motivate participants.		3	4	5
	Minimum points to pass 15			Pass?	Yes
	TOTAL				
	Total possible points 30				No
	POINTS				

Youth Character Development Toolkit

Parent/Guardian Documentation	Components	Not Exist	In Dev.	Exists Unclear	Clear Effect.
	Parental role is clearly defined.		1	2	4
	Parents receive regular progress reports.		1	2	4
	Parents are involved in program planning.		1	2	3
	Parents can actively participate in aspects of the program.		1	3	4
	Minimum points to pass 7			Pass?	Yes
	TOTAL				No
	Total possible points 15				
	POINTS				

Youth Character Development Toolkit

Value Experiences and Decisions Documentation	Components	Not Exist	In Dev.	Exists Unclear	Clear Effect.
	There is a written teaching plan in regard to character development.		2	4	8
	There is informal reinforcement of values activities by staff and/or students.		1	2	3
	There are clearly defined learning experiences and an understanding of how teaching should occur.		1	2	3
	Social rewards (formal and informal) are given for expected behavior.		1	2	3
	There are frequent discussions and explanations of behavior and consequences.		1	2	3
	Discipline is productive rather than demeaning.		1	2	3
	"Teachable moments" are recognized and used to instill character traits.		1	2	3
	There are celebratory "rites of passage" that clearly reinforce character elements.		1	3	4
	Minimum points to pass 15			Pass?	Yes
	TOTAL				No
	Total possible points 30				
	POINTS				

Youth Character Development Toolkit

Components	Not Exist	In Dev.	Exists Unclear	Clear Effect.
The program has identified "champions" for character development who also define the effort and desired outcomes.			1	2
Participants are included in determining the targeted benefits of the program.			1	2
Baselines are defined and progress measured.		1	2	4
There is clearly defined accountability for outcomes.		1	2	4
Other external organizations and/or templates are used to evaluate the program(s).		1	2	3
Minimum points to pass 7				
TOTAL		Pass?		Yes
Total possible points 15				No
POINTS				

Measurement Documentation

Youth Character Development Toolkit

Plan for Improvement Documentation	Components	Not Exist	In Dev.	Exists Unclear	Clear Effect.
	There is a defined quality assurance program.			1	2
	The participants' growth and the program's effectiveness are both measured and the findings used to improve the program.			2	3
	Assessment is focused on progress toward goals and includes input from staff, participants, parents, and the community.				1
	Measurement includes impact on other life skills such as academics.				1
	New methods are included/tested in measuring program effectiveness.				1
	Results are shared with other programs.				1
	There is comparative measurement from year to year or from one type of program to other programs.				1
	Minimum points to pass 4				Yes
	TOTAL			Pass?	
	Total possible points 10				No
	POINTS				

Youth Character Development Toolkit

Links with the Community Documentation / Components	Not Exist	In Dev.	Exists Unclear	Clear Effect.
Other community resources are used to reinforce efforts of the program.		1	2	3
There is regular communication between the program and community resources.		1	2	3
Multiple community-wide techniques are used to evaluate the participants and the program.			1	2
Lessons from the program are linked to daily living experiences.		1	2	4
The program(s) are directly linked with other community programs and there is shared governance and accountability.		1	2	3
Minimum points to pass 7				
TOTAL			Pass?	Yes
Total possible points 15				No
POINTS				

Youth Character Development Toolkit

Staff Involvement and Development Documentation					
Components	**Not Exist**	**In Dev.**	**Exists Unclear**	**Clear Effect.**
All regular staff are engaged in planning the program.			1	2
All regular staff participate in program evaluation.			1	2
All regular staff are included in staff development programs.				1
All regular staff are evaluated for their efforts in helping build character.			1	2
Time and resources are set aside for staff development.				1
Character development is often a topic of staff meetings.			1	2
Warm, supportive relationships are built between participants and staff.			1	2
Praise is the primary motivational tool.			1	2
Staff are actively involved in external character development organizations.				1
Minimum points to pass 7			Pass?	Yes
TOTAL				No
Total possible points 15				
POINTS				

Youth Character Development Toolkit

Summary and Comments Page: Number of sections passed _____ or **ALL** _____ TOTAL POINTS _____

Component	Comments
Mission Statement Defining documents 5/10	
Clear Value Messages and Responses 15/30	
Age Appropriate Teaching 15/30	
Modeling 15/30	
Parent/Guardian Involvement 8/15	
Value Experiences and Decisions 15/30	
Measurement 8/15	
Plan for Improvement 5/10	
Links with Community 8/15	
Staff Involvement and Development 8/15	

*Children are the living messages we send to a time
we will not see.*

John W. Whitehead

Men acquire a particular quality by constantly acting a particular way... you become just by performing just actions, temperate by performing temperate actions, brave by performing brave actions.

Aristotle

And finally...

You can tell a lot about a fellow's character by his way of eating jelly beans.

Ronald Reagan

www.ingramcontent.com/pod-product-compliance
Lightning Source LLC
LaVergne TN
LVHW081348060426
835508LV00017B/1469